English G 21

Klassenarbeitstrainer

für Schülerinnen und Schüler

mit Lösungen
Lerntipps

Cornelsen

English G 21 • Band B 6

Klassenarbeitstrainer mit Lösungen und Lerntipps

Konzeption
Dr. Ursula Mulla und Nogi Mulla, Germering

Erarbeitet von
Bärbel Schweitzer M.A., Staufen

In Zusammenarbeit mit der Englischredaktion
Dr. Christiane Kallenbach (Projektleitung)
Ulrike Berendt (verantwortliche Redakteurin), Doreen Arnold
Susanne Bennetreu, Stefanie Juhnke (Bildredaktion)

Beratende Mitwirkung
Helge Kipp, Mülheim an der Ruhr
Martina Schroeder, Stedtlingen

Tonaufnahmen
Clarity Studio Berlin

Bildquellen
Alamy, Abingdon (S. 6: Catchlight Visual Services; S. 10 li.: Juice Images (RF); S. 14: HA Photos (RF); S. 20: Image Source (RF); S. 27: Erik Palmer (RF); S. 37: David J. Green; S. 38: UpperCut Images (RF); S. 53: Glyn Thomas Photography; S. 54: Angela Hampton Picture Library); **Cinetext**, Frankfurt/Main (S. 22: Concorde); **Corbis**, Düsseldorf (S. 8: Ocean (RF); S. 47: Demotix/Demotix/Lois); **Getty Images**, München (S. 7 oben: Stockbyte; S. 10 re. unten: Wolfgang Weinhäupl (RF); S. 16: Peter Dazeley; S. 41: Daniel Schoenen/LOOK); **Randy Glasbergen**, Sherburne (S. 42 oben u. unten); **iStockphoto**, Calgary (S. 5 li.: kali9, 2. v. re. oben: corolanty, 2. v. li.: cortneyk, re.: SusanHSmith; S. 7 unten: Jasmin Awad; S. 9: apomares; S. 19: JohnnyGreig; S. 24 oben: VMJones; S. 33 li.: scanrail, re.: arratansi; S. 36 li.: laflor, re.: georgemuresan; S. 51 oben re.: yorkfoto, unten re.: hjalmeida, oben li. und unten li.: drbimages, Mitte li.: coloroftime); **Shutterstock**, New York (S. 4: Greg Epperson; S. 5 2. v. re. unten: wrangler; S. 10 oben: Trevor kelly; S. 13: Dmitri Mikitenko; S. 17: auremar; S. 21 li.: Shutterstock.com/s_bukley, Mitte: Shutterstock.com/Rena Schild, re.: Shutterstock.com/Featureflash; S. 24 unten: olly; S. 29: JustASC; S. 34 re.: ssuaphotos, Mitte: Yuri Arcurs, li.: Shutterstock.com/Stefan Glebowski; S. 35: MANDY GODBEHEAR; S. 43: Ustyujanin; S. 44: Vlue; S. 45 li.: juan carlos tinjaca, re.: Rui Vale de Sousa; S. 50: BigganVi; S. 57: Pojoslaw; S. 59: Simone van den Berg; S. 62: YanLev)

Textquellen
S. 25: Abridged and adapted from "Teens would rather lose TV than internet or mobile survey" by Charles Arthur. Copyright Guardian News and Media Ltd 2012; S. 39: Abridged and adapted from: http://eusew.eu/. (Stand: 29.5.2012); S. 41: Abridged and adapted from "Hermann will den Radverkehr verdoppeln." © dpa; S. 54–55: Abridged and adapted from: http://www.london.gov.uk/young-london/teens/have-your-say/yl-survey.jsp#2. (Stand: 10.6.2012). With special thanks to the Greater London Authority for permission to cite from the publication of the Young Londoners Survey.

Titelbild
Getty Images, München: (woman (M): Erik Isakson (RF))

Layout und technische Umsetzung
Heike Freund, Hameln

Umschlaggestaltung
Klein & Halm Grafikdesign, Berlin

www.cornelsen.de
www.EnglishG.de

1. Auflage, 3. Druck 2015

Druck: H. Heenemann, Berlin

ISBN 978-3-06-032991-5

PEFC zertifiziert
Dieses Produkt stammt aus nachhaltig bewirtschafteten Wäldern und kontrollierten Quellen.
www.pefc.de
PEFC/04-31-1156

INHALT

Klassenarbeiten, Vorbereitung auf die Prüfung, Prüfungen ...

... ist das 10. Schuljahr wirklich eine solch große Hürde?

Liebe Schülerin, lieber Schüler,

blickst du noch ein bisschen unsicher in das 10. Schuljahr? Denkst du mit gemischten Gefühlen an den Abschluss am Ende des Schuljahres?

Das ist ganz normal.

Das 10. Schuljahr ist ein gezieltes Hinarbeiten auf das Ende deiner Schullaufbahn. Mit intensiver Vorbereitung von Anfang an kannst du den Klassenarbeiten und dann auch der Prüfung gelassen entgegenblicken. Der Klassenarbeitstrainer unterstützt dich ganz gezielt bei der Vorbereitung auf die Klassenarbeiten.

Zu jeder Unit findest du zwei Klassenarbeiten, mit denen du alle Fertigkeiten (skills) trainieren kannst, die du für die Klassenarbeiten brauchst. In jeder Unit werden eine, manchmal sogar zwei Kompetenzen verstärkt geübt. In Unit 1 geht es gleich los mit dem Listening, in Unit 2 werden Reading und Mediation intensiver geübt und in Unit 3 ist das Writing mit zwei umfangreichen Aufgaben an der Reihe. In allen drei Units findest du zusätzliche Übungen zur Wiederholung wichtiger Grammatikkapitel. Du erkennst sie an dem Hinweis „REVISION +". Mit Abschluss der Unit 3 kannst du dann der Prüfung getrost entgegen blicken.

Wichtig ist, dass du dich den Herausforderungen der 10. Klasse stellst, indem du sie gezielt angehst und heute noch mit der Vorbereitung mit Hilfe des Klassenarbeitstrainers beginnst. Arbeite regelmäßig mit dem Klassenarbeitstrainer und überprüfe deine Ergebnisse sorgfältig mit dem Lösungsheft. Viele Aufgaben kannst du nach einiger Zeit auch ein zweites oder drittes Mal bearbeiten. Du hast dann die Möglichkeit, Probleme vom letzten Mal direkt anzugehen und dich so kontinuierlich zu verbessern.

Ich wünsche dir alles Gute und – auch wenn's manchmal mühsam ist – viel Freude beim Lernen.

Get started right away and be successful ...

Bärbel Schweitzer

Gesamtpunktzahl ______ / 113	Note ______

LISTENING

______ / 45

01 1 A radio phone-in – today's topic: How did you meet your partner?

______ / 26

a) *Read the task. Then listen to Lisa. Do the multiple choice tasks and tick the best answer to each question. (4P)*

1 Lisa talks about	a) her birthday and the day before.	
	b) her 20th birthday.	
	c) a man in her evening classes.	
	d) her birthday presents.	

2 The young man	a) used his credit card.	
	b) didn't want to have the money back.	
	c) was standing behind Lisa.	
	d) wanted to go to Lisa's party.	

3 Lisa and the young man	a) drank a bottle of French wine together.	
	b) started going out after her party.	
	c) want to get married soon.	
	d) want to have at least three children.	

4 After Lisa's story, the reporter says that	a) another person is going to tell their story.	
	b) there is a break now.	
	c) he liked the story.	
	d) they are going to play a love song.	

02 ***b)*** *Read the task. Then listen to Nick. Then answer the questions in a few words only. (6P)*

Notizen machen während des Hörens
Natürlich kannst du dir während des Hörens auch Notizen machen, um die Fragen im Nachhinein leichter beantworten zu können. Dazu musst du schnell schreiben können. Außerdem ist es gut, wenn du dir ein paar Abkürzungen überlegst, die du immer verwendest. Achte besonders auch auf Zahlen und schreibe sie mit.
Finde selbst heraus, wie du die Aufgaben besser lösen kannst: mit oder ohne Notizen.

1 Where did the girl live before she came to Bristol?

____

2 What did the boys do to impress her? *(Give 3 examples)*

____

3 Where did Nick and the girl meet one day?

____

4 Why did they work together?

____

5 How long had they been together?

____

6 How can you tell that they're still friends?

____

03 ***c)*** *Listen to Anna. Then complete the sentences. (8P)*

1 Anna got to know her boyfriend ______________________________

______________________________. *(Give 2 facts)*

2 Her cousin is from Germany, and her husband ______________________________.

3 Anna sat next to ______________________________.

4 The German boy ______________________________.

5 Their conversation got better when they ______________________________.

6 On the day after the wedding party ______________________________.

7 When Anna has finished college, she ______________________________.

04 ***d)*** *Listen to Leo. Then say whether the sentences are* ***right*** *or* ***wrong****.*
Tick the correct box. (5P)

	right	wrong
1 Leo had invited a friend to a dancing club.		
2 There were more boys than girls.		
3 Leo talked a lot to the nice girl.		
4 Leo had some problems with dancing.		
5 Perhaps Leo will go to the classes again.		

e) *Correct the wrong statements. You may listen again. (3P)*

____

____

____

____

____

05 2 At the café

___ / 19

a) *Read the sentences below. Then listen to the dialogue and put the sentences in the correct order. (8P)*

	A Jonathan has to go back to work.
	B Jonathan is sitting at a table in a café.
	C Catherine looks at adverts in the newspaper.
	D Catherine gives some information about her future plans.
	E Catherine comes into the café.
	F Jonathan gives some information about himself.
	G Catherine likes one of his ideas.
	H Jonathan has some suggestions for Catherine.

b) *Listen to the dialogue again. Then complete the mind map. (11P)*

About Jonathan

About Catherine

Why Catherine needs a part-time job

Jonathan's suggestions for a part-time job

Catherine's jobs so far

LANGUAGE

____ / 38

1 WORDS Me and my friends

____ / 8

Complete the text with words from Unit 1. The letters in the blue boxes will give you another adjective for a friend who is good and reliable.

I have many friends, boys and girls. Their a _ _ _ _ _ _ _ _ _ is different.

Most of them are quite t _ _ _, some have s _ _ _ _ _ _ _ hair,

only three of them have c _ _ _ _ hair. Some of the girls are really good-looking and

a _ _ _ _ _ _ _ _ _. I don't like a _ _ _ _ _ _ _ people,

so of course all of them are really c _ _ _ _ _ _ _.

Ah, you want to know some things about me too? Well, I think I'm a l _ _ _ _ _ _

person with a good s _ _ _ _ _ _ h _ _ _ _ _. I don't like working so

much so some people say that I'm l _ _ _. But I laugh a lot and I always talk to people

_ _ _ f _ _ _ _ _ _ _ w _ _. Normally I'm not nervous because

I have a lot of c _ _ _ _ _ _ _ _ in what I'm doing. P _ _ _ _ _ _

I should also m _ _ _ _ _ _ that I like to f _ _ _ _ with the girls.

2 GRAMMAR My friends and their hobbies

____ / 14

Lucy is talking about her friends. Complete the sentences with the ***simple present*** *or* ***present progressive****.*

Mara, one of my friends, ______________________ (love) taking photos. She always ______________________ (carry) her camera around. She ______________________ (not take) any photos of people, she always ______________________ (take) photos of nature. Here you can see her. She ______________________ (take) a photo of a flower.

Susan ______________________ (love) languages. At the moment she ______________________ (learn) Dutch. She ______________________ (speak) English, Spanish and Italian. She ______________________ (not speak) Portuguese but she also ______________________ (want) to learn German.

Here you can see Philip, Chris and Ava. They ______________________ (not like) watching TV, in fact, one of them even ______________________ (hate) it. Sometimes they ______________________ (watch) a film at the cinema. In this photo they ______________________ (play) one of their many board games.

☞ **Verwendung von simple present und present progressive**

Das **simple present** wird verwendet, wenn eine Handlung regelmäßig, oft oder nie geschieht. Es wird auch verwendet, um über Dauerzustände zu sprechen.

Das **present progressive** wird meist bei Handlungen verwendet, die in diesem Augenblick geschehen. Man nutzt es auch für die Beschreibung von Tätigkeiten auf Fotos oder Bildern.

	positive	**negative**
Simple present	I go, she goes, they go	I don't go, he doesn't go, they don't go
Present progressive	I'm going, she's going, they're going	I'm not going, he isn't going, they aren't going

3 GRAMMAR REVISION + A social day for Mike and his friends

____ / 16

Every year in autumn there is a "Community Day" in Mike's town. Everybody is encouraged to help make the town look nicer. Mike and his friends wrote an article for the local newspaper describing why they took part and what they did.

a) *Complete the sentences with* ***simple past*** *forms. Be careful: there is one* ***passive*** *form. (12P)*

"We had decided to join the 'Community Day' long before the actual day. We simply ________________ (want) to do something for our town. And we ________________ (think) it would be fun working together. It ________________ (be) our job to clean places inside and outside town. We ________________ (start) at the station where we ________________ (not find) a lot of rubbish. We ________________ (be) more successful when we ________________ (go) to the small river near our town. We ________________ (find) many different things: a lot of rubbish like paper, plastic and glasses, of course, but also a mobile phone, a watch and an old school-bag. After we had taken away all the rubbish, we ________________ (try) to find the owner of the mobile phone. As we ________________ (not be) successful in finding him or her, we ________________ (take) it to the lost property office. In the evening we ________________ (invite) to an Italian restaurant by the mayor of our town."

Verwendung von simple past und past perfect
Das **simple past** wird verwendet, wenn etwas zu einem bestimmten Zeitpunkt in der Vergangenheit geschah und das Geschehen abgeschlossen und vorbei ist.

Das **past perfect** drückt aus, dass etwas vor etwas anderem in der Vergangenheit stattgefunden hatte.

	positive	negative
Simple past	I went, I cleaned	I didn't go, I didn't clean
Past perfect	I had gone, I had cleaned	I hadn't gone, I hadn't cleaned

b) *Read the text again and find the two past perfect forms and underline them. Write a sentence to explain when the* ***past perfect*** *is used. Then write three sentences where you must use the* ***past perfect****. (4P)*

I use the past perfect when I want to show that ________________________________

____

1 ____

2 ____

3 ____

MEDIATION

____ / 14

Ein Freund, ein guter Freund

Deine Familie hat Besuch von einer Familie aus Frankreich. Jean, der 12-jährige Sohn der Familie, interessiert sich sehr für Filme und besonders für's Filmemachen. Ihr findet diese Ankündigung im Internet. Du erklärst Jean auf Englisch, worum es in dieser Ausschreibung zum Wettbewerb geht.

Gib folgende Informationen auf Englisch weiter:

1 *Erkläre das Thema „Ein Freund, ein guter Freund". Gib dabei mindestens zwei Beispiele, was in dem Film vorkommen könnte. (vier Fakten)*
2 *Was kannst du einschicken, um an dem Wettbewerb teilzunehmen? (drei Fakten)*
3 *Erkläre die Teilnahmebedingungen. (drei Fakten)*
4 *Informiere über die Jury und die Preise. (vier Fakten)*

Home | Über das Festival | Geschichte | Wettbewerbe | Kontakt

Ein Freund, ein guter Freund

Ein guter Freund ist viel wert. Überlege, was du mit deinen Freunden machen kannst und in welchen Fällen sie zu dir halten. Kannst du dich auf sie verlassen? Bist du selbst ein „guter Freund"? Wann hat dir ein Freund schon mal so richtig aus der Patsche geholfen? In einer Situation, in der dir sonst keiner mehr geholfen hat? Weißt du, wie es ist, wenn man z. B. von Klassenkameraden gemieden oder gehänselt wird?

In unserem nächsten Filmwettbewerb geht es genau um dieses Thema. Wie jedes Jahr suchen wir junge Regisseure, die einen Kurzfilm drehen.

Thema ist also: Mein bester Freund.

Was bedeutet es für dich, für einen Freund ganz da zu sein? Vielleicht hast du schon mal einem Freund geholfen, der Probleme mit seinen Eltern hatte? Oder hat dir schon mal deine beste Freundin geholfen, als du große Schwierigkeiten in der Schule hattest? Du kannst uns zeigen, wie du für einen Freund da bist oder wie dein Freund für dich da ist. Vielleicht möchtest du auch eine Geschichte über ein Tier erzählen, das dir besonders am Herzen liegt. Erzähle einfach drauf los.

Du hast mehrere Möglichkeiten, an dem Wettbewerb teilzunehmen:

Du kannst einen kurzen Film drehen, du kannst uns den Entwurf für einen Kurzfilm oder auch für einen Zeichentrickfilm aufschreiben.

Dein Film kann lustig, traurig oder verrückt sein – je nachdem was zu deiner Idee passt. Das entscheidest du natürlich selbst.

Wir jedenfalls freuen uns auf deine Idee.

Sie sollte bis zum 1. Februar bei uns in Passau sein. Die genaue Adresse findest du unter **Kontakt**.

Ein paar wenige Bedingungen gibt es, die du beachten solltest: Dein Film darf höchstens 4 Minuten lang sein, und du selber darfst nicht älter als 14 Jahre sein. Die Idee für den Film muss von dir stammen.

Die Jury besteht aus Erwachsenen und Jugendlichen. Der Film, der den ersten Preis gewinnt, wird auf dem Nationalen Filmfestival im Oktober gezeigt. Der Gewinner des 2. Platzes erhält 150 Euro, der 3. erhält 100 Euro.

Also, mach dich gleich an die Arbeit. Wir sind gespannt auf deinen Film!!!

1

2

3

4

WRITING

_____/ 16

How I got to know ...

The magazine "Young Friends" has asked its readers to write articles on how they got to know a special friend. Think of one of your friends and write an article of about 120–140 words. Use the ***simple past****.*

Write about
- *when, where and how you met your friend,*
- *what you thought or felt when you first met him/her,*
- *why you became friends.*

Gesamtpunktzahl ohne Speaking	____ / 78	Note ____
Gesamtpunktzahl mit Speaking	____ / 91	Note ____

READING

____ / 15

YFC – Young Film Competition

About us | The competition | How to enter | Tips | FAQs | Archive | Film academy

Do you like watching films?
Do you have some good ideas for a film?
Have you always wanted to make a film?
And – are you now looking for a chance to make your dream come true?

YES??? Then YFC is for you. We want to encourage young people from 12 to 22 to use their ideas to produce creative short films, short films for young Canadian people made by young Canadian people. That's why we organize a competition every year. Write and direct your film with our help.

We are not looking for finished films – no, we simply want to see your ideas. So show us an outline or a summary of your film idea or give us an idea of the first scenes of your film. It doesn't need to be perfect.

Your film ideas should be based on one of the following subjects:
- relationships,
- bullying,
- the environment.

It's our job to choose the ten best ideas. Our professional committee will check all the entries very carefully.

The ten film ideas will then be produced here in our film academy during four weekends in January and February. It's going to be a training process for you, our young film-makers. This process will include all the different aspects of film-making, for example directing the film, music, special effects. Don't be afraid, there will be professional film-makers to help you and to work together with you. There will also be students from our film academy who will be ready to give professional advice. Get as much or as little help as you like and need.

After the films have been made, there will be a film festival in June. The ten films will be shown to the public.

There will be discussions on the films and in the final celebration the ultimate winners will walk on the red carpet.

There will be awards for the three best films.

For more details about the festival events contact us at yfc@yfcfestival-film.com.

YFC asks for your entries not later than 10 October. If you need some more inspiration, look at the Archive of previous winners. Visit our 'How to ...', FAQs and Tips pages to get help entering the competition, then click the upload links below to get started!

We're looking forward to your ideas. Come on, get started right away!

a) *Three friends from Canada have heard about the film competition. They have many questions. Read their questions and then decide if they get an answer from the text. (12P)*

		Yes – there is an answer in the text	No – sorry, no answer in the text
1	Is it an international competition?		
2	Is any topic allowed?		
3	Can the three of us work together on one idea?		
4	At what age can we take part?		
5	How many pages do we have to hand in?		
6	Can we hand in two different ideas?		
7	Do we get any help from YFC?		
8	Will every film be produced?		
9	Will other people have the chance to watch the films?		
10	How many people took part in the last few years?		
11	What are the prizes?		
12	How can we find out more about the film festival?		

b) *Choose three questions and answer them with information from the text. (3P)*

LANGUAGE

___ / 50

1 WORDS About films

___ / 5

Complete the sentences with words and expressions from the box. Be careful: there are two more than you need.

are based on • award • bet • directed • recommend • review • reviewer • romantic • set in • special effects • stars • unfortunately

1 Many people read a ____________ about the film before they go to the cinema.

2 Sometimes films are different from the books that they ________ ________ ________.

3 Susan likes films with friendship and love, she likes ____________ films.

4 I love watching films ____________ by James Cameron.

5 People who are interested in history like films that are ________ ________ previous centuries.

6 Action movies are very cool, I like the ____________ ____________.

7 The Oscar is the most famous film ____________.

8 We can have a ________ on whether you'll like the film. Believe me: you'll love it.

9 Pete wanted to see this new film that ____________ Brad Pitt.

10 ____________, he broke his leg, so he couldn't go to the cinema.

2 WORDS Getting by in English

___ / 4

Sage, dass ...

1 ... Elly mit ihrem Freund Schluss gemacht hat.

____

2 ... du den Namen nicht verstanden hast.

____

3 ... Ann sehr arrogant ist, anders als ihr Bruder Adam, der sehr charmant ist.

____

____

4 ... du auch nicht zur Party gehst.

____

____

3 GRAMMAR A survey on young people

____ /7

Lucy and Frank did a project about what young people do in their free time. They interviewed three friends and wrote the results in a calendar. Look at the calendar. Then answer the questions below in full sentences and give the correct information if necessary.

A = meet friends
B = do homework
C = help parents
D = learn German vocabulary
E = play computer games
F = do sports
G = watch TV/DVDs

Monday	Tuesday	Wednesday	Thursday	Friday	Saturday	Sunday
Linn → A, B Dave → B, E Joe → F, G	Linn → A, B Dave → B Joe → F, E	Linn → B, D Joe → F, E	Linn → A Dave → B	Joe → F	Linn → A Dave → C, E Joe → F, G	Linn → A Dave → A

1 Does Linn ever do her homework on Thursday and Friday?

____

2 What does Linn usually do at the weekend?

____

3 What does Dave do twice a week?

____

4 What does Joe often do?

____

5 What do Joe and Dave never do?

____

6 Does Dave help his parents on Friday?

____

7 What do Dave and Linn both always do on Monday?

____

4 GRAMMAR REVISION + What will be in the future?

____ / 10

At the film festival there is an interview with the young film-maker Joanna. Fill in the missing forms of the ***will-future****.*

Interviewer We now have the chance to talk to one of our young film-makers here … So, Joanna, thank you for the exciting film about the two friends. Now, let's talk a bit about your future. What can you tell us about it?

Joanna Well, I hope I ____________________ (have) the chance to make many more films in the future, so that I ____________________ (be able to) learn more about film-making. I hope I ____________________ (go) to a film academy in the near future.

Interviewer We ____________________ (be) glad to see more of your films. I'm sure you ____________________ (make) other exciting films and ____________________ (be able to) go to the film acadamy. Are there any topics you are especially interested in and are there others you are not interested in, Joanna?

Joanna Well, I can definitely say I ____________________ (not make) any detective stories because I'm not interested in crime stories. I suppose I ____________________ (go on) making films about relationships, I think this is something people are always interested in.

Interviewer Many people ____________________ (be) happy to hear about your plans for more films. I'm sure you ____________________ (become) famous.

Joanna Thanks very much. I hope so too.

Interviewer Thank you and goodbye.

5 GRAMMAR REVISION + My ideas for the film

____ / 18

Stephen handed in a film idea for the film competition. Today he describes where he got the idea for the film from. Complete the sentences with the ***simple past*** *or* ***past perfect****.*
Be careful: there is one ***passive*** *form.*

I ______________________ (have) the idea for "Her Eyes" when I ______________________ (be) in the swimming pool last summer. Suddenly I ______________________ (see) this girl who ______________________ (not be) particularly pretty, but her eyes ______________________ (be) special. But I ______________________ (not talk) to her. After I ______________________ (leave) the swimming pool, I still ______________________ (think) about her eyes and ______________________ (start) making up a love story. First I ______________________ (not write) down anything, I just ______________________ (think) of ideas. But because I ______________________ (not write) down my ideas, I soon ______________________ (forget) them. So I ______________________ (decide) to write them on small pieces of paper. That ______________________ (be) a really good idea. After about three weeks I ______________________ (collect) all my ideas and I then ______________________ (write) down everything. The film ______________________ (produce) this year in February.

6 GRAMMAR REVISION + A backstage meeting

_____ /6

You have won a backstage meeting with a famous person. Choose a person you would like to meet.
It can be a famous singer, an actor, a politician, ...
You want to write an interview for the "Young Page" of your local daily newspaper.
The day before you go to the meeting you work out your questions. Think of six or more questions.

☞ Hilfe für die Bildung von Fragen findest du im Grammar File 2 auf S. 153 in deinem Englischbuch.

MEDIATION

___/13

Almanya – Willkommen in Deutschland

You have an English friend who is interested in the film "Almanya – Willkommen in Deutschland". Explain in English what the film is about and give the most important details.

Der sechsjährige Cenk Yilmaz fragt sich, ob er Deutscher oder Türke ist. Seine 22-jährige Cousine Canan erzählt ihm die Geschichte seines Großvaters und der Familie. Hüseyin kam als türkischer Gastarbeiter in den 1960er Jahren nach Deutschland und holte die ganze Familie nach. Canan berichtet von den Anfängen und dem Leben der Familie in Deutschland, von den Träumen und den Schwierigkeiten im fremden Land.

Eines Abends überrascht Großvater Hüseyin seine Familie mit der Nachricht, dass er ein Haus im alten Heimatdorf in der Türkei gekauft hat, das als Ferienhaus dienen soll. Die ganze Familie macht sich auf den Weg in die Türkei. Es begegnen ihnen viele Erinnerungen. Schließlich nimmt die Reise eine unerwartete Wendung und am Ende bekommt Cenk eine ganz besondere Aufgabe.

SPEAKING

___/13

06 An interview with a young film-maker

Listen to the interview between Luke from the radio station "Younger" and Neil, a young British film-maker. He is 22 today, but produced his first film when he was only 17. Listen carefully to what Mike asks. You can take notes if you want.

____

____

____

____

____

____

____

Now you

Today you have the chance to interview somebody. Find yourself a partner. Look at the two posters and information about two films on page 24 that were produced for the "Young Film Competition" festival. Choose a film. You take the role of the interviewer. Make some small talk and keep the conversation going. Your partner can answer your questions with the information given on page 24.

Find out about

- *the content of the film,*
- *the idea for the film,*
- *the production of the film,*
- *the film stars,*
- *plans for the future.*

Here are some phrases that may help you:

- Oh, that's interesting. Can you tell more about this?
- So you have ...
- Another thing that I want to ask you ...
- Well, this is ...
- Now one last question, ...

→

Content of the film:
Shows relationship between an old lady and her dog, shows the normal day of an old lady, lives alone in a small house, only has a dog
Shows getting up, feeding the dog, going for walks with the dog, shopping in the supermarket, Mrs Creek only talks to the dog, dog is her life, her best friend, doesn't need a TV because of the dog, is happy

Idea:
From her own grandma who has a dog and doesn't talk to many people during the day but is very happy

Making the film:
Was rather difficult because of the dog, grandma liked it very much, she loved being the main actor in the film

The film stars:
Grandma Elly and her dog Romeo

Plans for the future:
Only 12, no real plans for the future, first it's school, school, school, loves animals very much, maybe wants to become a vet

Content of the film:
Funny, gives information about how to save the environment, Robinia (mother) cares for environment, for example: pays much attention to rubbish, finds different ways to save energy, wants to make her family take care as much as she does (with funny actions)

Idea:
From a project at school (how to save energy, how to help the environment by small actions)

Making the film:
Directed the film and also acted, had clear ideas, professionals helped to realize them, added funny elements, had no idea about the music, but one of the film students added great sound tracks

The film stars:
Me (Samantha) as Robinia (mother), Rob (husband) and Cindy (daughter, 10 years old) (all of them friends of mine)

Plans for the future:
Most important: finish school, then film academy, later produce films, especially films about the environment

Gesamtpunktzahl ______ / 69 Note ______

READING

______ / 30

1 Teenagers and the media

______ / 19

The text about a survey on teenagers and their media is taken from the British newspaper "The Guardian".

New survey: Teenagers and their top three media

Young British teenagers would be less worried about doing without television than losing access[1] to the internet or their mobile phones, according to a new research.

Yet Britain's youngsters also watch more TV than at any time in the past five years, the survey found – though a growing amount comes through using online services such as the BBC's iPlayer. On average, they watch 17 hours 37 minutes per week, up from 15 hours 37 minutes in 2007.

Internet use has also become more popular, with 95% of 12- to 15-year-olds having internet access at home through a computer. But the research also points out that only 80% of children in lower social classes have access to the internet at home, compared to 98% in the richest ones.

A speaker from the survey said: "The almost universal use of the internet at home by 12 to 15s – both for their education as well as their entertainment – is a positive step forward."

The annual survey was carried out in spring with 1,717 in-home interviews, and focused on attitudes to communications technology by parents and children. It found that 28% of children aged 12 to 15 said they would most miss their mobile, and 25% would most miss the internet if it was taken off them – compared to only 18% who would miss television. A year ago mobile was the most desired with 31%, while TV was on the same level as the internet at 24%.

Radio listening is also becoming less popular, with around half of those aged 12 to 15 not listening to any sort of radio, according to the survey results.

Parents are increasingly taking more care of their children's online usage, with the living room being the most common location for internet use, although a third of 12- to 15-year-olds have internet access in their bedrooms. The majority of those aged 5 to 11 use the internet with an adult in the room, but usage alone increases with age: half of those aged 12 to 15 used the internet alone. However, that figure has fallen since last year.

"The research also shows that parents and children are increasingly aware of how to be safe when using the internet," said one of the speakers. "But risks do remain. Better understanding – amongst parents as well as their children – is the key to helping people to manage content and communications, enabling them to enjoy the benefits of media use while protecting themselves from the potential risks."

Smartphone usage is also growing: around half of all children aged up to 15 have their own mobile phone, and the proportion with a smartphone is growing fast, having risen from 36% a year ago to 46% now. The use of mobile phones generally is also growing strongly among children aged 8 to 11, rising from 55% a year ago to 61% now.

Games console popularity seems to have hit a plateau, at between 81% and 92% depending on age, though the figures are almost unchanged from a year ago.

[1] access ['ækses] *Zugang*

→

a) *Read the text and find the missing information. Write short answers only. (14P)*

1 Name two things about teenagers and TV.			
2 Give the percentage of children from lower classes who don't have access to the internet.			
3 Name two things teenagers use the internet for.			
4 Write down the percentage of children who would miss their mobile, the internet and the TV this year and last year.		this year	last year
	mobile		
	internet		
	TV		
5 Write down the number of teenagers who listen to the radio.			
6 Name the place in the house where most children use the internet.			
7 Write down percentage increase in children with a smartphone from last year to this year.			

Unbekannte Wörter erschließen

Um einen Text zu erfassen, brauchst du nicht jedes einzelne Wort zu verstehen. Es gibt aber unterschiedliche Möglichkeiten, ihre Bedeutung zu erschließen:

- In vielen Fällen ist es möglich, die Bedeutung unbekannter Wörter aus dem Zusammenhang zu erschließen, d.h. aus den Wörtern, die vor und nach dem zu erschließenden Wort stehen.
- Manche Wörter sind auch über die Kenntnis ähnlicher Wörter zu erschließen, z.B. kennst du das Wort „popular". „Popularity" ist das dazugehörige Substantiv und könnte im Textzusammenhang als Beliebtheit erschlossen werden. Allerdings musst du auf sogenannte „false friends" aufpassen. Das sind Wörter, die im Deutschen ähnlich aussehen wie im Englischen, aber trotzdem eine ganz andere Bedeutung haben, z.B. *I become, I will*.
- In vielen Fällen kannst du die Wörter auch über dir bekannte Wörter aus einer anderen Sprache erschließen, z.B. aus dem Französischen *historique, la politique*.
- Oft wird die Bedeutung von Schlüsselwörtern des Textes durch beigefügte Bilder klar.

b) *Finish the sentences with information from the text. (5P)*

1 Not all children have ______________________________.

2 The survey is carried out ______________________________.

3 More parents care about how their children use ______________________________.

4 Many younger children use the internet together ______________________________.

5 More than half of the children aged 8–11 ______________________________.

2 A do-it-yourself workshop

____/11

A do-it-yourself workshop

From our reporter Steve Collins in Brighton

Your bicycle is broken and you have no possibility to repair it? You need a new bicycle but have no money to buy a new one? You are looking for a special part for your bike? So read on and find out about a great new shop that has the answers to all these questions.

Emma's and Henry's bike workshop is just outside Brighton. There are many good reasons for people to come to the shop. It's the place to go to repair your bike. You can use all the equipment and you don't have to pay much to use it. If you need a new part for your bicycle you will find a second-hand part in the workshop. The bike workshop opened only a few months ago but it has already become a hit.

Emma told me it was originally her idea. She had seen bike workshops in Vienna, London and San Diego. Back home in Brighton she knew she wanted a bike workshop here too. But would such an idea work in the small town of Brighton? Would there be enough people wanting to repair their bikes themselves? Emma knew that it was a big risk. But one day she rented an old garage and volunteers (that's what friends are for!) helped her to renovate as cheaply as possible. Today it's a comfortable place where people enjoy working. Meanwhile the do-it-yourself workshop has become more and more popular, and Emma needn't worry about paying the rent any longer.

When Emma got to know Henry, a car mechanic, she knew immediately that he was the ideal person for her workshop. Today Henry offers courses for everybody. "You have to know how a bike works before you can repair it properly," he says. "So I teach people some basics about bikes before we start repair them. Most of the people who have taken part in one of my basic repairing courses come back to our place whenever there is something wrong with their bike. They like the atmosphere here and of course the fact that we have all the necessary tools here. You don't need to buy a single tool, you will find everything in our workshop." And as I found out, this is absolutely true.

Emma showed me all the different old bike parts. It's amazing what you can find there. "Sometimes there are people who want to make their own bike, you know, they want to make an individual bike with old parts they find here. Or they take parts from their old bike and add new ones from here. It's a way of recycling bikes really. And it's a way of reducing rubbish." Fantastic!

The customers of the bike workshop are of all ages and of all professions. Some are students, some are nurses or shop assistants, some are university professors. Most of them don't have the possibility to repair their bikes at home because either they have no place or they don't have the correct tools to do so. What they have in common is their love of their bikes. So if you want to meet bike lovers, just go along and meet them there. And you will definitely meet me too!

→

a) *Read the text and tick the correct ending. (6P)*

1 Customers come to the bike workshop	a) when they are looking for a new bike.	☐
	b) when they have a problem with their bike.	☐
	c) when they are looking for somebody to repair their bike.	☐

2 Bike workshops	a) can also be found in other cities.	☐
	b) are always a big risk.	☐
	c) are run by people for their friends.	☐

3 Emma wasn't sure	a) if she really wanted a bike workshop.	☐
	b) if her friends would help to renovate the garage.	☐
	c) if she could earn enough money with the bike workshop.	☐

4 Henry	a) repairs the bikes.	☐
	b) thinks that people must get to know their bikes.	☐
	c) likes the atmosphere in the bike workshop.	☐

5 Emma is sure that	a) the bike workshop helps the environment.	☐
	b) everybody can make his or her individual bike with many different parts.	☐
	c) the author of the article will find the missing part he is looking for.	☐

6 Most of the customers	a) don't have much money.	☐
	b) would prefer to repair their bikes at home.	☐
	c) are bike fans.	☐

b) *You have read the article and decide to go to Brighton and meet Emma and Henry.*
Ask them ***five*** *questions about their work in the bike workshop. Use different questions forms. (5P)*

____

____

____

____

____

LANGUAGE

____ / 29

1 WORDS From the newspapers

____ / 6

Fill in the correct words from the box. Put them in the correct form if necessary. There are two more than you need.

amount of • carbon footprint • climate • discovery • emission • fossil fuel • global warming • household • insulation • invention • medicine • power • scientist • target

1 Since 1970 British ____________ have needed about 34% more energy. Use gadgets that save energy!

2 The latest figures show that UK ____________ fell by 7% in 2011.

3 Will Britain reach its ____________ and reduce its ____________?

4 The ____________ of a new ____________ might help the fight against AIDS.

5 Because of the warm winter, less ____________ was needed in Britain.

6 A Brighton high school student is proud of his new ____________. Look at his solar barbecue.

7 The ____________ of the town hall will cost more than expected.

8 ____________ is the most complicated environmental problem the world has to solve.

9 Greenhouse gases are mainly produced by burning ____________.

10 The ____________ carbon dioxide produced rose again.

2 WORDS A crossword

___ / 4

Complete the crossword with the missing words from the sentences.

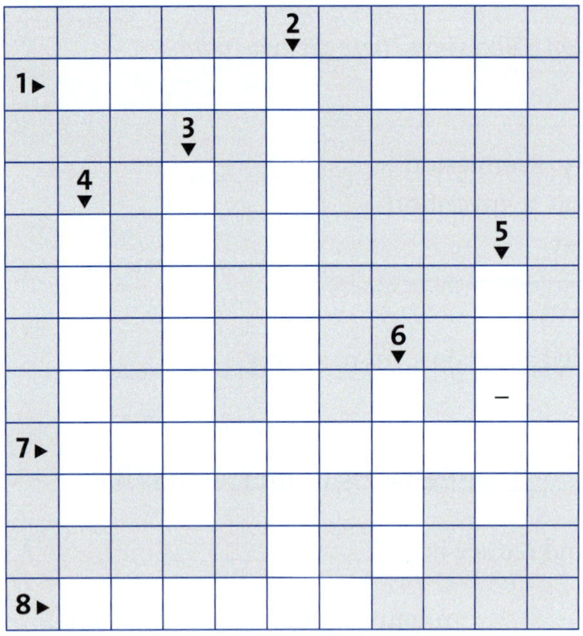

Across

1 I couldn't use the washing machine yesterday because there was a ... between 2 and 5 pm.

7 There are really good living ... around here.

8 I looked at my friend's kitchen the other day. Believe me: there is a ... for almost everything in her kitchen.

Down

2 You are also ... for our environment and you have to try to save energy. It's not only "the others" who have to take care.

3 I don't like people who only ... to care about the environment but don't do anything to save it.

4 My parents want to buy a new car. They have the ... between a normal one and an electric car.

5 Having the heating on while the window is open is a ... .

6 We have to pay a lot of money for gas this month. The ... is very high.

3 GRAMMAR REVISION + My bike is repaired

_____ / 11

a) *Complete the sentences with the correct form of (to)* ***be able to****, (to)* ***be allowed to****, (to)* ***have to****.*
You can choose from the box. (6P)

was able to (2x) • had to • was allowed to • wasn't able to • have to

can – may – must und ihre Ersatzverben
Modale Hilfsverben (können/dürfen/müssen) können nicht alle Zeiten ausbilden, deshalb gibt es Ersatzverben.

	Present	Past	Future
können	can/be able to	could/was/were able to	will be able to
dürfen	may/can/be allowed to	could/was/were allowed to	will be allowed to
müssen	must/have to	had to	will have to

Wenn du dir unsicher bist, dann lies dir vor der Bearbeitung der Aufgabe noch einmal das Grammar File 8 auf S. 161–162 in deinem Englischbuch durch.

Adam Have you got a new bike? Your old one is broken, isn't it?

Oliver I _____________________ afford a new one, so I repaired my old one.

Adam I don't believe it! Did you repair it yourself?

Oliver Yes, I did. I _____________________ do it with the help of the bike workshop down the road.

Adam Hey, it must be new. I haven't heard of it.

Oliver Yes, it is. It's great! I went there with my broken bike. A young man showed me round and then I _____________________ use all the tools they have.

Adam What about new parts?

Oliver Ah, good question. You don't have to buy expensive new parts. They have hundreds of used parts, and you simply look for the part you need. Of course, you _____________________ pay for it. I also _____________________ pay for using the workshop at the end, but believe me, it was a fair price. I _____________________ pay it from my pocket-money.

b) *Think about going by bike, bus or car. Write* ***five*** *sentences using (to)* ***be able to****, (to)* ***be allowed to*** *and (to)* ***have to****. Use them in different tenses. (5P)*

____

____

____

____

____

4 GRAMMAR REVISION + About the environmental projects

____ / 8

a) *There have been many projects at Westland School during the last few months. Many of them have to do with the environment.*
*Tick the correct **relative pronoun** or **pronouns**. Also tick "not necessary" when you can leave the relative pronoun out. (5P)*

> **Relativpronomen**
> Relativsätze beziehen sich auf ein Nomen und bestimmen dieses näher.
> Bei Personen verwendest du die Relativpronomen **who** oder **that**, bei Dingen **which** oder **that**.
> Wenn das Relativpronomen Objekt des Relativsatzes ist, kann es auch weggelassen werden.
> Wenn du noch unsicher bist, kannst du im Grammar File 10 auf S. 164 in deinem Englischbuch weitere Hilfen finden.

	who	which	that	not necessary
Mr Sunderland is the teacher ____________ asked us what project groups we would like to work in.	✔		✔	
1 The project were we plant trees is the project ____________ I like best.	☐	☐	☐	☐
2 Look, there is the girl ____________ is in the same project as me.	☐	☐	☐	☐
3 The head teacher is talking to the students of the project ____________ deals with the pollution of the air.	☐	☐	☐	☐
4 Sue and Carmelita are the two girls ____________ I work with in my project.	☐	☐	☐	☐
5 Alan is the one ____________ is responsible for painting the posters in his project.	☐	☐	☐	☐

b) *Write **three sentences** with two different relative pronouns. (3P)*

1 ____

____

2 ____

____

3 ____

____

WRITING

___ / 10

Gadgets on class trips

Read the following letter of an English head teacher to the parents and students of his school.
What do you think about banning mobile phones and MP3-players from school trips?
Is it OK or are there reasons why these gadgets should be allowed?
Write your opinion in about 120–150 words.

Dear students and parents,

Next week we are going on our class trip. Therefore we would like to remind you of our school rules. Please make sure that the students do not take their mobile phones and MP3-players with them.

Many thanks.

Regards,

Andrew Johnson, head teacher

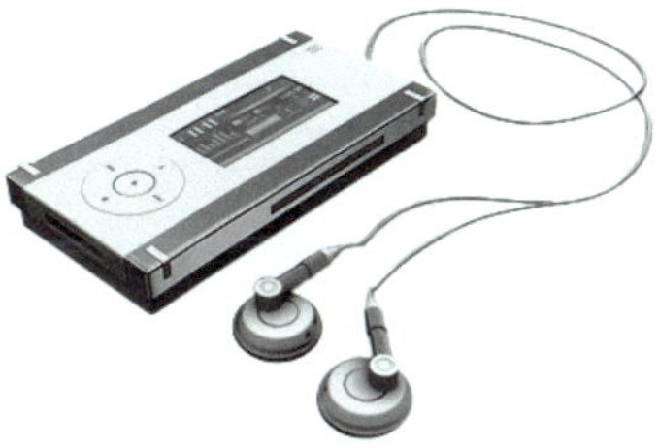

Klassenarbeit B

Gesamtpunktzahl ohne Speaking	______ / 103	Note	______
Gesamtpunktzahl mit Speaking	______ / 129	Note	______

LISTENING

______ / 22

07 1 Talking about the environment

______ / 8

a) *Listen to the text and complete the sentences. (4P)*

Bei diesem Hörtext musst du dich auf viele Zahlen einstellen.

One person in a car on a trip of 300 miles produces __________ kg CO_2.

One person on a plane on a trip of 300 miles produces __________ kg CO_2.

Four people in a car on a trip of 300 miles produce __________ kg CO_2.

Four people on a plane on a trip of 300 miles produce __________ kg CO_2.

b) *Complete the sentences with information from the text. (4P)*

1 Many people prefer flying because it's ______________________________ and it

____

2 A longer trip by car can be cheaper than flying if ______________________________

____

3 If you use public transport, emissions are ______________________________

____

2 A family discussion

_____/ 14

08 ***a)*** *Listen to the discussion. Then do the multiple choice task and tick the correct statements. (4P)*

1 Dad	a) tells his kids that he is going to sell the family car.	
	b) wants to make a difference and help the environment.	
	c) wants to get fit.	
	d) wants to go by bike.	

2 Sarah	a) sees a problem with the shopping.	
	b) is 17 years old.	
	c) wants to take a taxi to get home after a party.	
	d) wants to go on holiday by car.	

3 Sarah	a) doesn't like Chris's idea.	
	b) wants to have driving lessons with her father.	
	c) wants her father to give her a car as a birthday present.	
	d) worries that she cannot take all her suitcases with her when they go on holiday.	

4 Chris	a) likes his father's idea.	
	b) would like to use public transport.	
	c) wants to go on holidays by plane.	
	d) only has some information about another car sharing system.	

→

b) *Who says what? Read the following statements and decide if they are part of Dad's or Chris's idea for the car sharing system. Write the names after the statements.*
Be careful: one statement is correct for both systems. (10P)

Dad

____

Chris

____

1 In this system, you can register online.

2 In this system, you sell your own car.

3 In this system, people can rent your car.

4 In this system, you book a car on the internet.

5 In this system, you don't pay tax and insurance for the car.

6 In this system, you keep your own car.

7 In this system, you only pay when your car is rented by somebody.

8 In this system, the registration doesn't cost anything

9 In this system, you become a member of the organization.

10 In this system, you set your own rates.

LANGUAGE

____ / 40

1 WORDS The environment

____ / 6

a) Collect at least six new words that have to do with the word field "environment". (3P)

climate, ______________________________

____

____

*b) Choose three words from **a)** and write a sentence for each one. (3P)*

____

____

____

2 GRAMMAR REVISION + An old woman is talking about cars

____ / 18

*Complete the sentences with the **simple present** or **simple past**.*

I can remember the times when nobody in our village ____________ (have) a car. And I still ____________ (remember) the day when the first car ____________ (drive) down the main street in our village. That ____________ (be) around the year 1938. Everybody ____________ (run) into the street when the car ____________ (come) nearer. It ____________ (be) an attraction for everybody. Our family ____________ (not have) a car until 1955. My sister and I ____________ (be) very proud when our father ____________ (arrive) in front of our house with the new family car. Today it's different. Almost every family ____________ (have) a car, some even ____________ (have) two. But things change: there are people who ____________ (not want) a car. They ____________ (use) public transport because it is cheaper and it ____________ (help) the environment. I ____________ (sell) my car ten years ago when I was 80. And I ____________ (give) my driving licence to the town hall on the same day. Today I ____________ (take) a taxi when I need to go somewhere.

3 GRAMMAR REVISION + A project for parents and young people

___ / 16

*Read the text and decide if you have to use the **active** or **passive**. Circle the correct form.*

There was an interesting project at Seaview High School last weekend.

The day **announced** / **was announced** on the internet as a hands-on day for children and their parents.

The police **wanted** / **were wanted** to inform the families about the dangers of the internet and how they can **protect** / **be protected** themselves.

A policeman **talked** / **was talked** about safety on the internet and **gave** / **was given** many examples of what can **be done** / **do**. Parents and children **ask** / **were asked** to tell the others about their experience with the internet.

A second very important topic was social networking sites because they **use** / **are used** by more and more teenagers. Children **asked** / **were asked** what they do first when they come home after school. They **answered** / **were answered** that they **communicated** / **were communicated** on social networking sites for more than half an hour.

"The internet **gives** / **is given** you a lot of freedom but it also **is taken** / **takes** people's time," the policeman **said** / **was said**.

During the workshop the parents had to do several tasks. Many of them **helped** / **were helped** by their children. At the end, everybody **was invited** / **invited** to ask questions, and the policeman **were answered** / **answered** them patiently.

MEDIATION

___/24

1 An energy day

___/12

Ein Freund hat von EUSEW gehört und die Idee, einen solchen Energietag zu organisieren, fasziniert ihn. Beantworte seine Fragen auf Deutsch.

About us | Our Energy Goals | Energy Day | Projects

EUSEW – Organize your Energy Day

Every year hundreds of organizations and individuals in over 30 countries take part in EU Sustainable[1] Energy Week (EUSEW) by hosting Energy Day events and activities that promote energy efficiency and renewable energy sources.

Be a part of it this year by holding a sustainable energy-themed event, project or activity in Brussels or in your country between 18 and 22 June.

An energy day is a non-profit[2] making event, project, exhibition or display. It must take place between 18 and 22 June (weekends before or after are also acceptable).

To become an official EUSEW host, simply register your Energy Day. We expect to have more than 500 hosts across 30+ countries! Don't delay. Create a EUSEW account and register your Energy Day activity today.

Organize your Energy Day!

Be part of a European movement to promote energy efficiency and renewable energy by organizing an Energy Day. Get visibility for your organization, city or region and spread best practice. Get new members and read about your activity in the newspaper.

Submit your Energy Day!

(You will be asked to create an account before you can register your Energy Day activity.)

Who are we?

The EU Sustainable Energy Week is an initiative of the European Commission in Brussels. Since 2006 hundreds of organizations and individuals have taken part in the EUSEW. They organize Energy Day events and activities that promote energy efficiency and renewable energy sources.

→

[1] sustainable [sə'steɪnəbl] *nachhaltig* [2] profit ['prɒfɪt] *Verdienst*

Tim Was steht da eigentlich über die EUSEW?

Du ______________________________

____

____

Tim Können wir das auch hier bei uns in Sachsen machen oder geht das nur in Brüssel?

Du ______________________________

Tim Ist das nun eine Woche oder ein Tag, den wir organisieren sollen?

Du ______________________________

Tim Und es muss genau in der Zeit vom 18.–22. Juni sein? Da haben wir doch unsere Parisfahrt.

Du ______________________________

Tim Also gut, ich stell mir vor, wir könnten da was mit unserem Fußballverein machen und uns nebenbei etwas für die Vereinskasse verdienen. Was meinst du?

Du ______________________________

Tim Was für einen Nutzen hätten wir dann für unseren Verein überhaupt? *(3 Fakten)*

Du ______________________________

____

____

Tim Das ist natürlich auch gut. Und was müssen wir tun, wenn wir mitmachen wollen?

Du ______________________________

____

2 Get on your bike

_____ / 12

Your English penfriend visits you for a few days. He is very interested in environment protection and has seen this newspaper article. He asks you to explain its content to him in English.

Regierung in Baden-Württemberg will Radverkehr verdoppeln

Stuttgart. Die grün-rote Regierung in Baden-Württemberg will den Radverkehr fördern. „Unser Ziel ist es, den Radverkehr in großen und kleineren Städten innerhalb von zehn Jahren zu verdoppeln“, sagt ein Sprecher der Regierung.

Kernpunkt des Projekts „RadKultur“ ist, für stärkere Akzeptanz des Fahrradfahrens zu sorgen. Ein Expertenteam von „RadKultur“ wird in den nächsten Monaten Vorschläge machen, wie das Radwegnetz ausgebaut werden kann.

Die Initiative „Radkultur“ wird zunächst in Tübingen, Lörrach und Mannheim umgesetzt. Zunächst denkt man an Ideenwettbewerbe und will mit gezielten Aktionen an Schulen für das Rad werben. Später will man auch Unternehmen als Partner gewinnen, denn auch Firmen müssen lernen, das Fahrrad zu akzeptieren.

Die Regierung stellt in den nächsten Jahren mehrere Millionen Euro zur Verfügung, um den Radverkehr im Alltag zu fördern.

Explain
- the government's target for the next years (2P)
- the initiative „RadKultur“ (4P)
- where and how the initiative will be realised (4P)
- why companies take part in the initiative (2P)

____

____

____

____

____

____

New words
Expertenteam *team of experts;* akzeptieren *(to) accept*

WRITING

___/17

A car of your own?

Many young people at the age of 20–25 don't want a car of their own.
What's your opinion? Would you like a car of your own once you have a driving licence?
Write a text of about 160–200 words.

Think about
- *costs*
- *your carbon footprint*
- *time*
- *...*

Einen Text strukturieren
Dein Text sollte in drei Hauptabschnitte eingeteilt sein:
- in eine Einleitung, die in das Thema einführt,
- in einen Hauptteil, in dem du deine Argumente zu den einzelnen Punkten vorbringst,
- in einen Schluss, in dem du deine eigene Meinung schreibst.

SPEAKING

____ / 20

09 How ecology-minded are we?

Look at the cartoon and try to understand its message. Then listen to the CD.

"Explain to me again why our ecology textbook is printed on dead trees."

Now you

Look at the cartoon and try to understand its message. Then talk about the cartoon.

Divide your talk into four parts:
- *first describe the cartoon,*
- *say what the cartoon is about and talk about the message,*
- *give your opinion about the message.*
- *Finally, talk about yourself and your family. What do you do to keep your carbon footprint low?*

SHOES

"We have a new line of environmentally-friendly shoes. They leave a low-carbon footprint."

Klassenarbeit A

Gesamtpunktzahl ______ / 110 Note ______

LISTENING

_____ / 26

Great success for students

10 ***a)*** *Read the table below. Then listen to the radio show and complete the table. (14P)*

1 Name the months when timetables change.	
2 Give information about the experience with the timetable changes so far. *(2 facts)*	
3 Say when the listeners found out that the bus company had reacted to the protests?	
4 Give reasons why the bus company reacted.	
5 Give two facts about where Steve lives.	
6 Name three reasons why the new timetable was bad for Steve.	
7 Name three ways the new timetable affected Melissa.	
8 Explain why Melissa thought that the bus company's timetable changes were not OK.	

11 ***b)*** *Listen to the second part of the radio show. Then answer the questions. You don't need to write complete sentences. You can listen twice. (12P)*

1 How does the school teach the students democratic rules?

___

2 What activities did they decide on in class? *(3 facts)*

___

___

___

3 What were the reactions to the students' activities? *(3 facts)*

___

___

___

4 Why was the protest a good experience for the students?

___

5 What has impressed Mrs Miller? *(4 facts)*

___

___

___

___

LANGUAGE

____/53

1 WORDS Creating new words

____/19

a) *Find words from the same word family. The words can be adjectives, verbs or nouns. Sometimes you might even find two words. (5P)*

independent	*independence*
1 true	
2 poor	
3 (to) think	
4 (to) annoy	
5 sense	
6 (to) apologize	
7 (to) feel	
8 (to) speak	
9 concentration	
10 (to) immigrate	

b) *Use four of the words you found in* ***a)*** *in the following sentences. (2P)*

1 The ____________________ of some London families is so alarming that the London authority[1] wants to help them.

2 I like Sam's new girlfriend. But yesterday she didn't tell the ____________________ when we talked about her last job.

3 Last month the Mayor of London talked to the public about his future plans. His ____________________ was fantastic.

4 My boyfriend really hurt me last week. Now I'm waiting for his ____________________.

c) *Write two more sentences with words you found in* ***a)****. (2P)*

____

____

[1] authority [ɔːˈθɒrəti] *Autorität, hier: Behörde*

2 GRAMMAR REVISION + A discussion about bus times

____ /9

*Before, during and after the students' campaign against the new bus times there were/are a lot of discussions. Here are some of the statements. Complete the **if-clauses** with the correct form of the verb in brackets.*

if-clauses – kurze Wiederholung

1	If	we	**go**	to London,	we	**will visit**	Madame Tussauds.
2	If	she	**had**	more time,	she	**would go**	to Paris.
3	If	I	**had invited**	her,	we	**could/would have talked**	to her.

Before the campaign

1 I ______________________ (have to) catch the early bus at 7.10 if I want to be at school on time.

2 If the bus company ______________________ (not change) the times, we will go on strike.

3 I ______________________ (not be able to) take part in the dancing lessons any more if I don't get home until 5.20 pm.

During the campaign

1 If we ______________________ (talk) to the bus company, perhaps they would change the times again.

2 We could inform a lot of people in town if we ______________________ (go) to the market square on Saturday morning.

3 If we ______________________ (collect) a lot of signatures from people in town, we could give them to the bus company.

After the campaign

1 If all the students had accepted the new bus times, some of them ______________________ (not have) time for hobbies after school.

2 If the students ______________________ (not write) the letter to the newspaper, the public wouldn't have known about the issue.

3 If the students hadn't done such a good job, the bus company ______________________ (not react).

3 GRAMMAR Teens speak out

____/10

Complete the newspaper article by choosing the right expression for the numbered gaps.
Tick the answers in the table below.

Students had the chance to discuss problem issues

"Teens Speak Out" – 1 – last Saturday morning with a short speech and an explanation of Rule No. 1: "You adults out there – 2 – to speak now," presenter Phil Cross told the audience.

During the discussion, students shared their opinions – 3 – many different topics. They – 4 – about communication with teachers and the head teacher, the importance of sports and about school safety.

14-year-old student Alan said that it was necessary to improve contact with the head teacher.

"The only time you hear from the head teacher is – 5 – an assembly, or when she's addressing all the students, or when there's something going on that she – 6 –," he said.

Sue, aged 15, agreed. She wanted the head teacher to see and recognize the good work that – 7 – by many students. "It's time the head teacher changed something. At the moment she only speaks to us when something is going wrong. Things would be much better if she – 8 – the good work and talked – 9 – the students about their – 10 –."

1	begins	began	begin	has begun
2	cannot	allow	aren't allowed	has
3	with	to	over	about
4	speaks	spoke	had spoken	will speak
5	during	while	on	with
6	don't like	will like	like	doesn't like
7	do	is done	did	has done
8	would see	saw	sees	doesn't see
9	to	at	about	on
10	succeed	successful	success	succeeded

4 GRAMMAR REVISION + Word order

______ / 8

Here are some notes from a students' meeting. Put the words in the correct order and write them down.

Die Wortstellung im englischen Satz
Bevor du mit dieser Übung beginnst, solltest du dir die wichtigsten Punkte zur Satzstellung im englischen Satz ins Gedächtnis rufen, z. B. S - V - O. Wenn du noch unsicher bist, kannst du auch im Grammar File 1 auf S. 152 in deinem Englischbuch nachlesen.

1 great meeting / had / last week / we / a /.
2 for the School Yearbook / first of all, / a picture / took / we /.
3 the school shop / was / long discussion / then / a / about / there /.
4 enjoy / all the students / things / nearly / buying / at the shop /.
5 heard / we / what / like / needs / they / to be improved / and / what /.
6 the youth club / after that / talked / we / about /.
7 to finish / didn't have / unfortunately, / the discussion / time / we /.
8 we / next Saturday / so / meet again / going to / are /.

1 ______________________________
2 ______________________________
3 ______________________________
4 ______________________________
5 ______________________________
6 ______________________________
7 ______________________________
8 ______________________________

5 Everyday English: Solving conflicts

_____ / 17

You are staying at a youth hostel in Sweden for a week. Ten people use the same kitchen, so everybody needs to tidy up after cooking and eating their meal.

A girl, Anna, has left the kitchen in a complete mess for the third time. As you want to use the kitchen now, you decide to talk to her. Make up a dialogue.

You	▶ start the conversation	Excuse me, Anna, can I have a word with you?
You	▶ name the problem	
Anna	▶ disagree that there is a problem and start talking about how wonderful your dinner was	
You	▶ explain the problem again	
Anna	▶ apologize, find a way to solve the problem	
You	▶ accept the apology and make a suggestion	
Anna	▶ accept the suggestion	

WRITING

____/31

1 Young people and their attitude towards the internet

____/15

Young people who are very involved in different projects in their free time, have been asked about using the internet. First read the young people's statements.

The internet is definitely not safe. I'm worried that personal information might be misused.

Surfing the internet a lot means you don't have enough time to get involved in useful projects, e.g. volunteering to help others.

The internet costs a lot of money, and you can't concentrate any longer on things that really matter.

Using the internet is too expensive.

The internet is only for relaxing.

→

You have been asked to write an article for your school homepage.
You have to think about the question: "Do young people need the internet?"

Write an article of about 170 words.

- *Start with an introduction explaining the young people's statements about the internet.*
- *Give some information about the statements. You need not write about all of them.*
- *Give your opinion:*
  - *What do you use the internet for and how often?*
  - *Do you agree with any of the statements? Why/Why not?*
  - *What do you personally think about the internet?*
- *At the end, sum up your arguments.*

Wichtige Punkte beim Writing:

- ☐ Beachte die Aufgabenstellung genau, du kannst wichtige Hinweise auch unterstreichen.
- ☐ Vor dem Schreiben: Sammle Ideen (z. B. mit einer Mindmap).
- ☐ Strukturiere den Text (Einleitung, Hauptteil und Schluss).
- ☐ Verwende **linking words** (**time phrases**, Konjunktionen, Relativpronomen).
- ☐ Beachte die Rechtschreibung und Grammatik (richtige Wortstellung, Zeiten).
- ☐ Achte auf eine sinnvolle Länge der Sätze.

2 A letter to the newspaper about a youth club

___ / 16

You are an exchange student in Bristol. At the moment there is a discussion about a new youth club. In last week's newspaper different opinions were discussed. Some people think that young people will only take drugs in the youth club and this is why they are against it. Others are afraid that too many teenagers from other towns will come to the new youth club.

On the other hand, many parents and many teenagers hope that the youth club will be opened soon. They think it is a good chance for young people in Bristol.

You are a member of a youth club team in Germany and your experience so far has been very good. This is why you want to support the Bristol youth club.

Write a letter to the newspaper. Write about 150 words.

In your letter give information about
- *who you are and where you are from,*
- *why you are writing this letter,*
- *the experience you had in Germany with the youth club (possibilities for all kinds of activities ▸ give examples),*
- *possible problems (alcohol, drugs, ...),*
- *one or two reasons why the youth club could be a great help for Bristol.*

Begin and end your letter in a suitable way.

Klassenarbeit B

Gesamtpunktzahl ohne Speaking ______ / 61	Note ______
Gesamtpunktzahl mit Speaking ______ / 82	Note ______

READING

______ / 11

Report on young Londoners

Nicolas has found a report on young Londoners on the internet.

a) *Read the information about the report and then answer the questions. You don't have to write complete sentences. (4P)*

In spring 2009, the Greater London Authority[1] organized a survey to find out more about young Londoners. The report covers young people's views on key topics such as education, crime and safety, getting involved in London, transport and the environment, and their attitudes to the main activities organized by the Mayor of London.

The results paint quite a positive picture of young people's lives in London, but also highlighted a number of significant problems which have to be solved.

More than one thousand young Londoners aged 11–16 took part in interviews between March and April 2009.

The survey was done to help us understand where we, the Greater London Authority together with the Mayor of London, can best offer our support to young people.

We also want to compare the results to the ones from the 2004 survey. And we want to use the results again in the future to find out what has been improved.

Abridged and adapted from: http://www.london.gov.uk/young-london/teens/have-your-say/yl-survey.jsp#2

1 What were four of the topics of the survey?	
2 Who was interviewed *(2 facts)*?	
3 Why did they need the 2004 survey?	

[1] Greater London Authority *Gesamtverwaltung für Groß-London*

***b)** Nicolas has taken some notes about the report. Read the notes and tick the correct statements on p.56. (7P)*

Active and involved

Young Londoners are getting involved:
55% have taken part in at least one activity to support a change in their area.
More should be done to activate young people:
51% of those that haven't taken part say it's because no one has asked them.
Only 7% that haven't taken part say it's because it wouldn't make a difference.

Feeling safe

83% of young Londoners feel safe in their neighbourhood – up from 77% in 2004.
Young Londoners' biggest worries are violent crime, and their own safety:
27% feel unsafe because of knife crime.
22% feel unsafe because of possible attacks in the street.
22% feel unsafe because of teenagers hanging round.

Crime and feeling safer

A minority, but significant number, report having been victim to violent crime:
1% (or 5,000) report being a victim of knife crime.
5% (or 25,000) report being a victim of attacks in the streets.
39% of young Londoners said 'more police' would make them feel safer – the top answer. This fits with young Londoners saying that 'safety and not enough police' is the 'worst thing' about London.

Education, skills & jobs

Young people feel more positive about the quality of their schools.
94% say their school is good or very good.
London has opportunities, even in difficult times.
70% of young Londoners are confident, even now, that London can give them the job opportunities they want.

Taking part in decisions

In general young Londoners feel they can do something about decisions in their schools, but not in their neighbourhoods or London.
67% feel they can do something about school decisions (10% more than in 2004).
31% feel they can do something about neighbourhood decisions.
16% feel they can do something about London's decisions.

London's environment

Young people think environmental issues are less of a problem now than they were in 2004, but the problem still exists.
Around 8 out of 10 saw climate change, traffic pollution and rubbish as a problem.
Around 7 out of 10 saw pollution of rivers, air pollution and death of plants and animals as a problem.
Saving parks and green spaces is the No 1 priority for improving London's environment: 32%.
Waste and air quality were also important issues.

Getting around

Buses are young Londoners' main form of public transport:
64% use them every day, or every other day.
The Zip Card (which gives free bus fares to under-16s, and some under-18s) does not keep young Londoners from walking to school:
38% often walk to school – the same number as in 2004.

London as a place to live

Young Londoners are happy with where they live – 85% think their neighbourhood is OK, 84% are happy with London as a whole.
Young people enjoy many different people
37% named the 'mix of people that live here' as the 'best thing' about London, second only to the 'many different shops'.

→

1 When talking about living in London, shopping	a) is the most important thing for young Londoners.	
	b) only comes second.	
	c) is not mentioned.	

2 The 2009 survey shows that	a) most young Londoners have tried to change something in their area.	
	b) it's necessary to activate more young people.	
	c) many young people think you can't change anything by getting involved.	

3 If you compare the results of 2004 and 2009,	a) in 2004, fewer young people said that they could take part in decisions at schools.	
	b) more people felt safe in 2004.	
	c) issues about the environment were not a problem in 2009.	

4 When talking about safety and crime,	a) many young people say that they have been victim to violent crime.	
	b) teenagers hanging around is one of the biggest problems.	
	c) many young Londoners would like the police to be more present in London.	

5 The survey says that	a) most young people walk to school although they could use the bus for free.	
	b) young Londoners don't walk because of the Zip Card.	
	c) the bus is the favourite form of transport.	

6 When talking about the environment,	a) young Londoners make it clear that parks are very important.	
	b) waste and air quality are the most important issues.	
	c) more young people mentioned the pollution of the waterways as a problem than rubbish.	

7 Many young people think	a) that the quality of their schools could be better.	
	b) that they will find a job in the London area.	
	c) that London cannot provide good opportunities in difficult times.	

LANGUAGE

____/39

1 WORDS Have your say – a discussion

____/6

Complete the text with the correct words from the box. Make sure you use the correct form. Be careful: there are three more than you need.

(to) accept • annoying • campaign • (to) charge • issue • (to) make sense • mosquito device (4x) • petition • politician • presenter • public • unless

Next week: Have your say – a discussion

The next ____________________ discussion on important local topics will be held on Wednesday, 7 July at 7.30 pm. This time the discussion will be on the ____________________ which has been installed in front of the youth club. As usual, interesting guests will take part and discuss the topic, for example Mr Pit Hank, a ____________________ here in our town. Mr Hank thinks the ____________________ is a useful thing and that it ____________________ where it is. Then there are Tom and Nicholas, two students who have started a ____________________. Tom and Nicholas don't want to ____________________ the ____________________ in front of the youth club any longer. And there is Mrs Felder. Although Mrs Felder lives near the youth club, she supports the ____________________ against the ____________________. Also there will be Mr Jeff Saltman who says that the mosquito device can't be removed ____________________ the young people get a new place to meet. Peter Smith, the well-known ____________________ from Radio Young, will lead the discussion.

Place: Grattan's Hotel, 24 Swansea Road.

2 WORDS Students talking in a school break

____/6

Circle the correct preposition.

1 I think Jo is very good **at** / **in** presenting topics.

2 I'm afraid **of** / **for** failing our Maths test tomorrow.

3 Mrs Sutter is a really good teacher. Her attitude **towards** / **with** the students is excellent.

4 I can't blame anybody else **to** / **for** my bad mark in English – I have just been too lazy the last few months.

5 I'm glad that Sue apologized **with** / **to** me **at** / **for** her bad behaviour.

6 I read in the school magazine that the number of hours spent **on** / **for** homework at our school has risen **at** / **by** ten per cent in the last two years.

7 I don't think that Mr Gardener is prejudiced **at** / **against** any of the students, he's very fair.

8 John is really interested **for** / **in** German history, he knows so much!

9 Mark will throw a big party **at** / **on** Friday evening.

10 Did you know that Mrs Sutter is married **to** / **with** a Swiss man?

3 WORDS Explaining words

____/7

Explain these words.

Explaining words
Worterklärungen benötigt man, wenn ein Gesprächspartner ein bestimmtes Wort oder einen Ausdruck nicht versteht oder man selber nach einem Wort sucht. Hier sind einige Hilfen:
- Oft kannst du ein Wort mit seinem Gegenteil oder einem Synonym erklären.
- Du kannst deine Erklärung mit folgenden Ausdrücken beginnen: **it's something ..., it's a person who ..., it's a place where ...,**
- oder aber du bettest das Wort in zwei bis drei Sätze ein, so dass die Bedeutung klar wird. Achte dabei auf korrekte Sätze.

1 fare	
2 (to) tell the truth	
3 equal	
4 (to) immigrate	
5 (to) complain	
6 tax	
7 likely	

4 GRAMMAR REVISION + About Ann's presentation

_____ / 9

a) *Complete the sentences with words from the box. Decide if you need an* ***adjective*** *or an* ***adverb*** *and complete the sentences with the correct form. Be careful: there are two more than you need. (6P)*

careful • easy • equal • fantastic • good • nervous • personal • simple

Adjective or adverb – kurze Wiederholung
Das Adjektiv erklärt näher, wie etwas oder jemand ist: **He is clever.**
Das Adverb erklärt näher, wie etwas gemacht wird: **He solved the problem cleverly.**

1 I think she was a bit ______________________.

2 She had prepared her presentation ______________________.

3 Ann talked in a way that I could follow her presentation ______________________.

4 ______________________, I liked the way she kept looking at the audience.

5 The outline was worked out ______________________.

6 The photos she showed were ______________________.

b) *Finish the sentences. Write down whether you have to use an* ***adjective*** *or an* ***adverb****. (3P)*

1 The presentation was ______________________. (ad__________.)

2 She talked too ______________________. (ad__________.)

3 I think people liked listening because the topic was so ______________________. (ad__________.)

5 GRAMMAR REVISION + Talking about the future

____/11

Über die Zukunft sprechen – welche Zeit muss ich verwenden?

- Du möchtest ausdrücken, dass etwas für die Zukunft geplant ist?
  ▸ *going to-future*
- Du möchtest ausdrücken, wie etwas in der Zukunft sein wird?
  ▸ *will-future*
- Du möchtest ausdrücken, dass etwas für die Zukunft fest verabredet ist?
  ▸ *present progressive*

Wenn du dir noch unsicher bist, lies noch einmal im Grammar File 5 auf S. 157 in deinem Englischbuch nach. Dort findest du weitere Beispiele.

a) *Complete the sentences with the* ***going to-future***, ***will-future*** *or* ***present progressive***. *(8P)*

1 Look, here is the ticket for my flight. I ____________ (fly) to Spain tomorrow.

2 Lisa has just given me a call. I think she ____________ (be) late for dinner.

3 I'm sorry, mum. I haven't had time to tidy up my room. I ____________ (do) it after school. I promise!

4 Nick's just told me about his problems at school. We ____________ (talk) to the teachers in a few days.

5 It's terribly cold, isn't it? But it ____________ (be) warmer next week.

6 It's Sue's birthday in a few days. I ____________ (send) her a nice birthday card.

7 We've already booked our holidays for next year. We ____________ (go) to Florida again.

8 This year Susanna was chosen to play the main part in the school theatre production. I'm sure that next year it ____________ (be) you, Alice.

b) *Now write three sentences about the future. Use the* ***going to-future***, ***will-future*** *and* ***present progressive***. *(3P)*

1 ____

2 ____

3 ____

MEDIATION

____/11

Have your say on Highway 2A

Im Unterricht behandelt ihr das Thema Bürgerbeteiligung. Du hast diesen Artikel über ein Bürgerbeteiligungs-projekt in Australien online gefunden und möchtest in der Schule darüber berichten.

Gib folgende Informationen auf deutsch wieder:

1 *Was die Verkehrsbehörde und die Gemeinde tun.*
2 *Worüber die Bürger befragt werden.*
3 *In welcher Form das Treffen stattfindet.*
4 *Wie die Bürger sich anmelden können.*
5 *Wie sich Bürger noch beteiligen können. (2 Fakten)*
6 *Wie die Bürger vorinformiert wurden.*

Road Services (RMS) are doing a report on the safety of Highway 2A at the moment.

Our citizens can have their say on the dangers of Highway 2A as part of a community workshop on Friday.

The community workshop forms part of the Northern Highway Road Safety review, and will be held between 10.30 am and 12.30 pm at Bay Waters Inn.

To register for the workshop, call Aretha on (067) 8866 5915. Roads Services (RMS) have said the phone number for residents wanting to register is now active.

People can also comment online using a special tool to show the locations where there are possible dangers, and make comments by emailing vista@highwayproject.com.

Notices were given to households along the Northern Highway, advertising the public meeting, and noting the phone number to register.

SPEAKING

____ / 21

12 At the end of school

Mittelberg Realschule has asked students in their final year to have their say about their school.
Listen to Paul talking about his six years at Mittelberg Realschule.

Now you

You are leaving school soon. Have your say about your school.

Talk about

- *How did you feel when you started at this school?*
  - *Were you excited, worried, happy?*
  - *What did you like about school, what didn't you like?*
- *How did your school life go on in years seven and eight?*
  - *Was it the same as in the years before?*
  - *What changed?*
- *How were your last two years? Talk about*
  - *your aims,*
  - *successes,*
  - *bad times,*
  - *the last few months at school.*
- *At the end, sum up your time at school and, if possible, give some advice on how the school should develop. Are there any tips you would like to give younger students?*

How to do well in a test

Countdown zum Testerfolg

Ein Test ist angekündigt? Kein Grund zur Panik. Wichtig ist, dass du weißt, worauf du dich vorbereiten musst. Im Zweifelsfall frag deine Lehrerin oder deinen Lehrer. Der Countdown kann beginnen!

Eine Woche vor dem Test

1 Lies noch einmal die **Texte** der zuletzt durchgenommenen Unit (A-Section und Text, eventuell auch das Background File). Fasse mündlich oder schriftlich zusammen, worum es ging.

2 Wiederhole den **Wortschatz** der Unit mit Hilfe des *Vocabulary* oder des *Wordmaster*. Schreibe dir die Wörter und Wortverbindungen, die du immer wieder vergisst, auf ein Blatt Papier. Eine Mindmap oder ein Wortfeld helfen beim Behalten.

3 Geh auch noch mal die neue **Grammatik** durch. Aufgaben zur Selbstüberprüfung und zum Üben findest du im *Practice*-Teil, auf der Seite „How am I doing?“, im *Grammar File* (S. 150–169), in deinem *Workbook* und im *e-Workbook*.

Zwei Tage vor dem Test

1 Wiederhole den **Wortschatz**. Manche Wörter sitzen noch nicht? Schreibe einen kurzen Text, in dem du sie verwendest.

2 Lies die **Texte** ein weiteres Mal.

3 Erkläre einem Freund oder einer Freundin die neue **Grammatik**. Das klappt nicht richtig? Dann lies nochmal im *Grammar File* nach.

Am Abend vor dem Test

1 Entspanne dich. Du kannst lesen, dich in die Badewanne legen, Musik hören, fernsehen, ...

2 Geh zur gewohnten Zeit ins Bett.

Am Morgen des Tests

1 Steh rechtzeitig auf, damit du nicht hetzen musst.

2 Lies irgendetwas „zum Aufwärmen“, aber schau nicht mehr in dein Schülerbuch.

Während des Tests

1 Denk daran: Du hast dich gut vorbereitet. Es gibt keinen Grund, nervös zu sein.

2 Konzentriere dich auf den Test, lass dich nicht ablenken.

3 Lies dir die Aufgaben genau durch. Dann löse zuerst die Aufgaben, die dir einfach scheinen. Wende dich erst danach den schwereren Aufgaben zu.

4 Aufgaben, die du bearbeitet hast, hakst du ab. So siehst du, wie du vorankommst, und behältst den Überblick.

5 Schau ab und zu auf die Uhr. Du solltest dir für den Schluss noch etwas Zeit einplanen, um deine Antworten noch einmal durchzulesen und wenn nötig zu korrigieren.

Aufgabenstellungen verstehen

Bevor du anfängst, die Aufgaben zu bearbeiten, vergewissere dich, dass du genau weißt, was du tun sollst. Lies die Aufgabe Wort für Wort langsam und gründlich und von Anfang bis Ende durch. Du kannst besonders wichtige Teile der Aufgabenstellung unterstreichen und die Aufgabe, wenn nötig, für dich in einzelne Schritte unterteilen.

Den folgenden Arbeitsanweisungen begegnest du häufig:

Add Verbinde eine Information oder einen Sachverhalt mit einer/einem anderen auf die geforderte Art und Weise.

Choose Wähle zwischen verschiedenen Möglichkeiten die passende Information aus.

Comment Kommentiere einen Sachverhalt durch die Darstellung deiner eigenen Meinung dazu. Begründe und erläutere sie möglichst genau.

Compare Vergleiche Dinge, Wörter oder Sachverhalte, indem du prüfst, ob und auf welche Weise sie gleiche oder verschiedene Eigenschaften, Aussehen, Bedeutungen oder Funktionen haben.

Complete Ergänze eine Information, indem du sie an dem dafür vorgesehenen Platz einträgst und damit z. B. einen Satz sinnvoll beendest.

Describe Beschreibe ein Objekt oder eine Person, d.h. stelle dar, wie sie aussehen, wie das Objekt funktioniert oder die Personen handeln. Vermeide eigene Wertungen wie z. B. „beautiful", „useful" oder „great".

Discuss Diskutiere ein Thema, eine Behauptung oder eine Aussage. Untersuche möglichst viele Seiten davon, z. B. Vor- und Nachteile, und stelle diese geordnet dar.

Explain Erkläre einen Sachverhalt, d. h. gib wesentliche Fakten über ihn und erläutere, wie sie logisch zusammenhängen.

Fill in Trage die geforderten Informationen in den dafür vorgesehenen Platz ein, z. B. in eine Lücke oder eine Tabelle.

List Schreibe einzelne oder mehrere Informationen übersichtlich und geordnet auf, z. B. in einer Reihe, Tabelle oder einem anderen Verzeichnis.

Listen Höre dir einen Text, einzelne Informationen oder Sachverhalte an.

Match Ordne die angegebenen Informationen einander zu, wie es die Aufgabe erfordert. Finde z. B. Satzanfänge und passende Satzenden und füge sie zusammen.

Use Verwende eine Tatsache, ein Wort usw. so, wie es in der Aufgabe gefordert wird.

Write a ... Schreibe etwas in einem geforderten Textformat auf, z. B. deinen Kommentar zu etwas oder eine Geschichte.